THIS NOTEBOOK BELONGS TO

________________________________

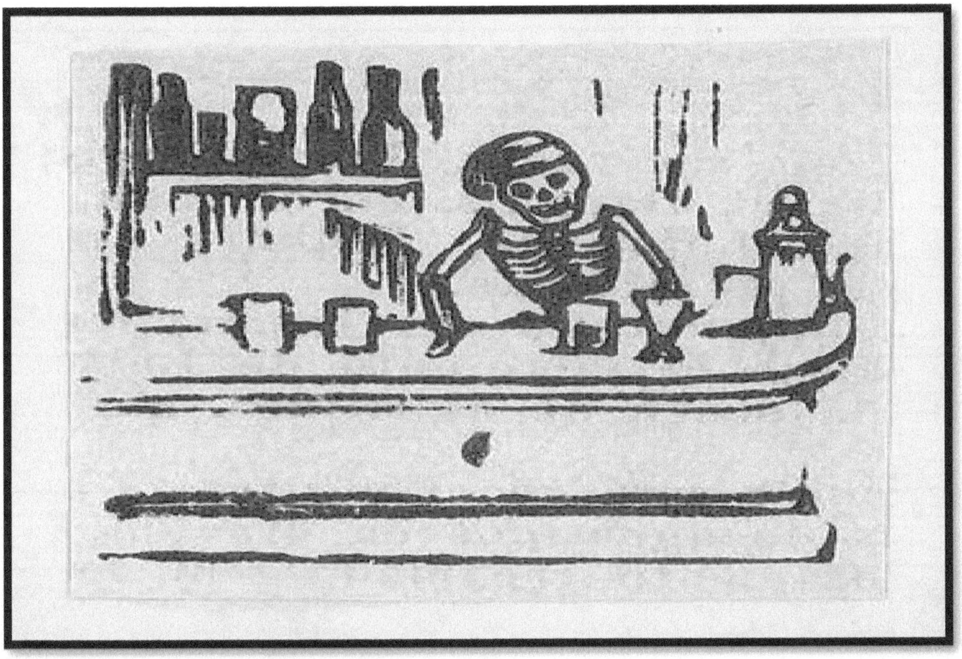

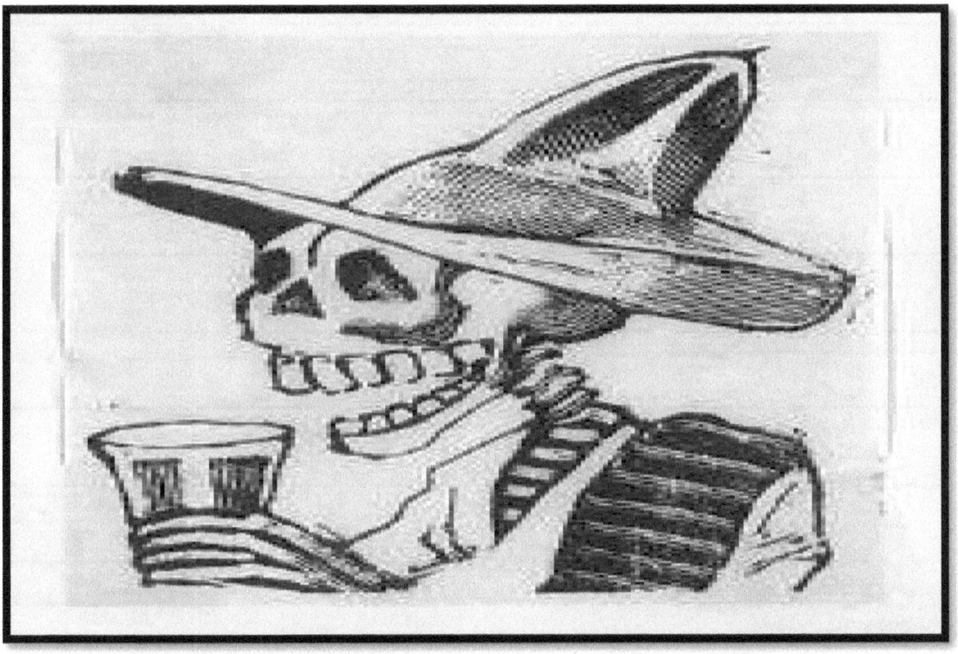

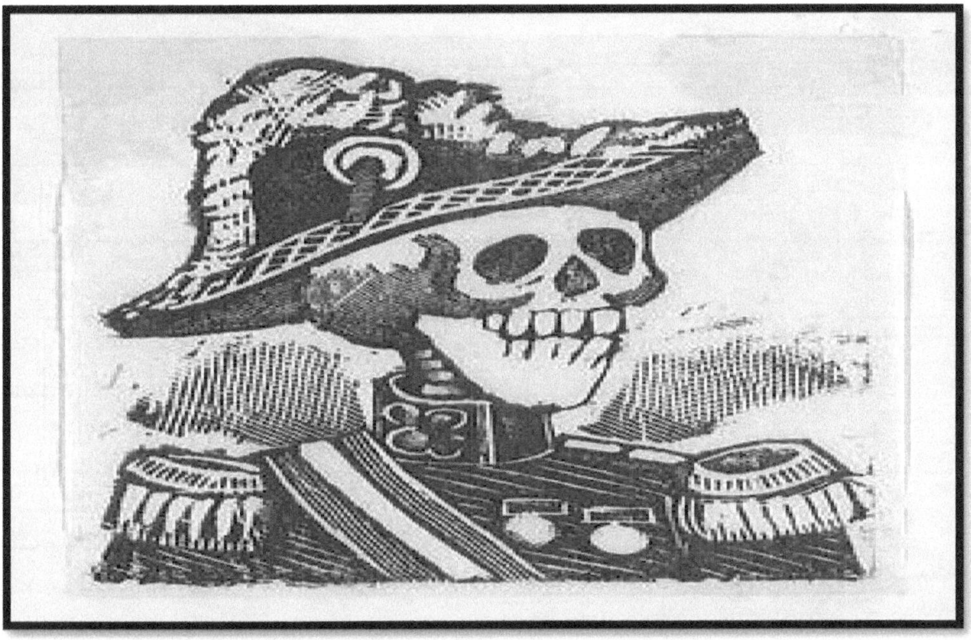

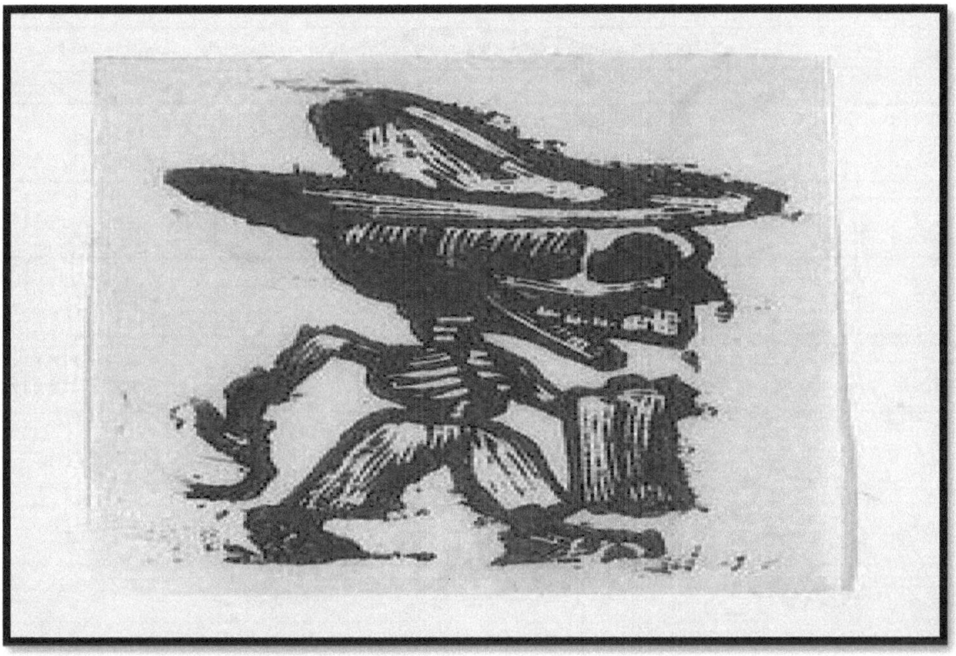

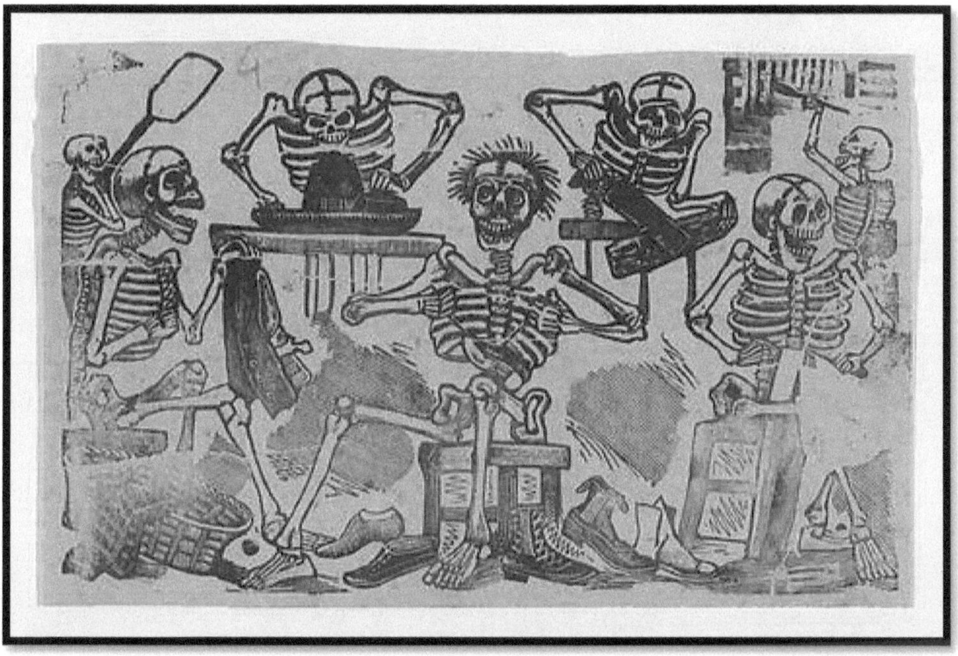

www.ingramcontent.com/pod-product-compliance
Lightning Source LLC
Chambersburg PA
CBHW030947240526
45463CB00016B/1982
* 9 7 8 1 6 9 7 9 1 0 9 7 1 *